ELITE MILITARY UNITS

HARLEM HELLFIGHTERS

Elite Infantry Soldiers of World War I

by Myra Faye Turner
illustrated by Orlando Caicedo

CAPSTONE PRESS
a capstone imprint

Published by Capstone Press, an imprint of Capstone
1710 Roe Crest Drive, North Mankato, Minnesota 56003
capstonepub.com

Copyright © 2026 by Capstone. All rights reserved. No part of this publication may be reproduced in whole or in part, or stored in a retrieval system, or transmitted in any form or by any means, electronic, mechanical, photocopying, recording, or otherwise, without written permission of the publisher.

Library of Congress Cataloging-in-Publication Data is available on the Library of Congress website.

ISBN: 9798875215827 (hardcover)
ISBN: 9798875215773 (paperback)
ISBN: 9798875215780 (ebook PDF)

Summary: Discover the true story of the Harlem Hellfighters, one of the most courageous and decorated all-Black military units of World War I. Despite facing discrimination in the United States and across the globe, the Harlem Hellfighters earned a reputation as fierce fighters on the battlefield. Follow their journey from New York to the front lines in France during WWI, where they proved their valor and changed the way the world viewed Black soldiers.

Editorial Credits:
Editor: Donald Lemke; Designer: Jaime Willems;
Production Specialist: Katy LaVigne

Image Credits:
Getty Images: duncan1890 (map background), back cover and throughout, spxChrome (old paper), cover and throughout; U.S. National Archives: 4

Any additional websites and resources referenced in this book are not maintained, authorized, or sponsored by Capstone. All product and company names are trademarks™ or registered® trademarks of their respective holders.

Printed and bound in the USA. 6307

Table of Contents

Harlem Hellfighters..................................... 4

Chapter One:
The Great War 6

Chapter Two:
Basic Training 10

Chapter Three:
The French Connection 14

Chapter Four:
Furious Fighters 20

More About the Harlem Hellfighters
of World War I...28
Glossary..30
Read More...31
Internet Sites 31
About the Author 32
About the Illustrator 32

HARLEM HELLFIGHTERS

Unit Name:
369th Infantry Regiment

Nickname:
Harlem Hellfighters

Origin:
Harlem, New York City, with soldiers from other parts of the United States

Years of Service:
1917–1919

Key Mission:
Fought alongside the French Army on the Western Front in World War I (1917–1918)

What They're Known For:
– First all-Black regiment to serve with the American Expeditionary Forces during World War I

– Fought in key battles, such as the Meuse-Argonne Offensive, Château-Thierry, and the Second Battle of the Marne

Awards:
170 soldiers were awarded the Croix de Guerre, France's highest military honor

Distinguished Member:
Henry Johnson, who single-handedly fought off a German raid and saved his fellow soldiers, was awarded the Medal of Honor in 2015.

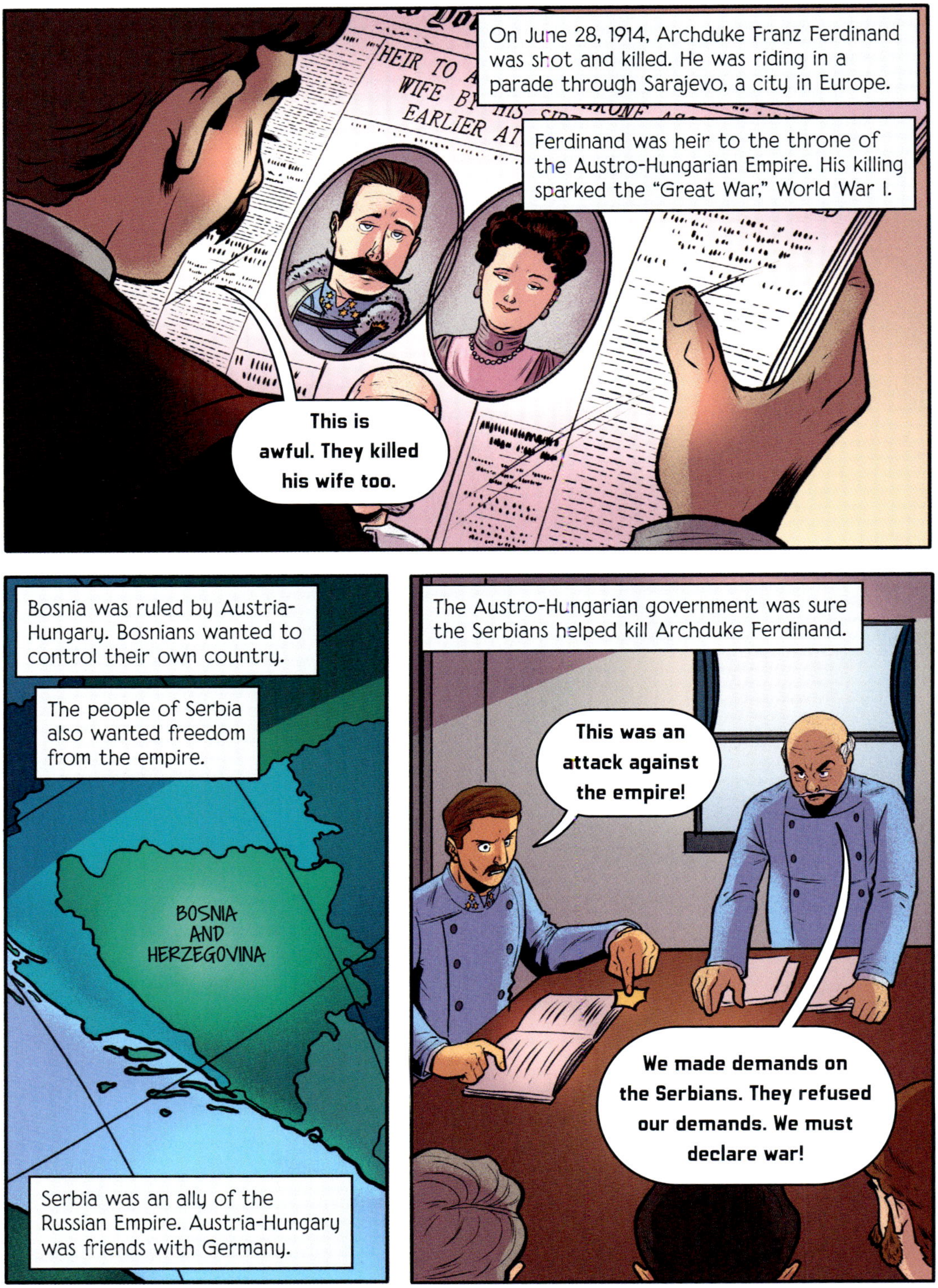
On June 28, 1914, Archduke Franz Ferdinand was shot and killed. He was riding in a parade through Sarajevo, a city in Europe.
Ferdinand was heir to the throne of the Austro-Hungarian Empire. His killing sparked the "Great War," World War I.
This is awful. They killed his wife too.
Bosnia was ruled by Austria-Hungary. Bosnians wanted to control their own country.
The people of Serbia also wanted freedom from the empire.
BOSNIA AND HERZEGOVINA
Serbia was an ally of the Russian Empire. Austria-Hungary was friends with Germany.
The Austro-Hungarian government was sure the Serbians helped kill Archduke Ferdinand.
This was an attack against the empire!
We made demands on the Serbians. They refused our demands. We must declare war!

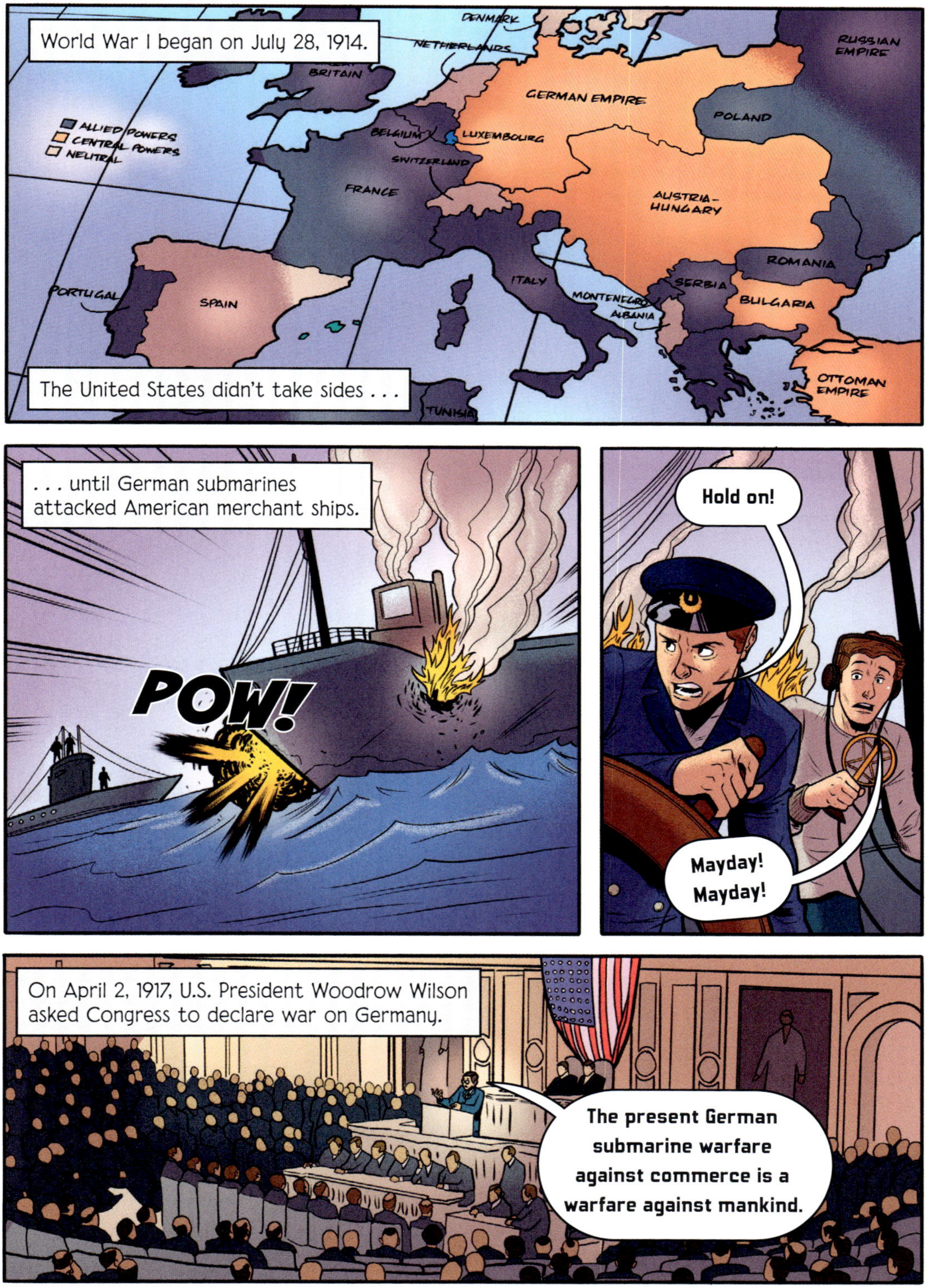
World War I began on July 28, 1914.
DENMARK
NETHERLANDS
BRITAIN
RUSSIAN EMPIRE
GERMAN EMPIRE
POLAND
ALLIED POWERS
CENTRAL POWERS
NEUTRAL
BELGIUM
LUXEMBOURG
SWITZERLAND
FRANCE
AUSTRIA-HUNGARY
ROMANIA
PORTUGAL
SPAIN
ITALY
SERBIA
BULGARIA
MONTENEGRO
ALBANIA
OTTOMAN EMPIRE
TUNISIA
The United States didn't take sides . . .
. . . until German submarines attacked American merchant ships.
POW!
Hold on!
Mayday! Mayday!
On April 2, 1917, U.S. President Woodrow Wilson asked Congress to declare war on Germany.
The present German submarine warfare against commerce is a warfare against mankind.

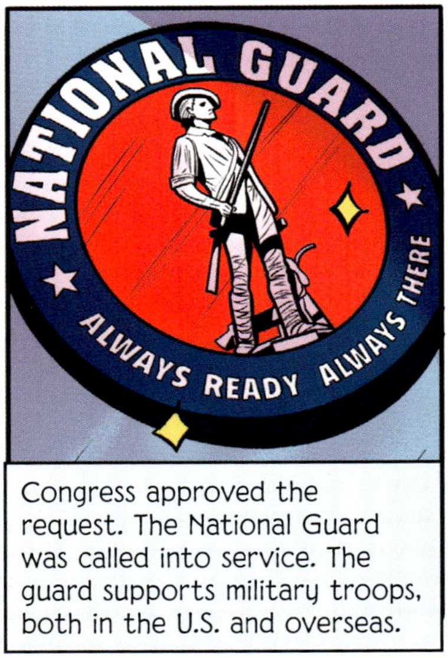
NATIONAL GUARD
ALWAYS READY ALWAYS THERE
Congress approved the request. The National Guard was called into service. The guard supports military troops, both in the U.S. and overseas.

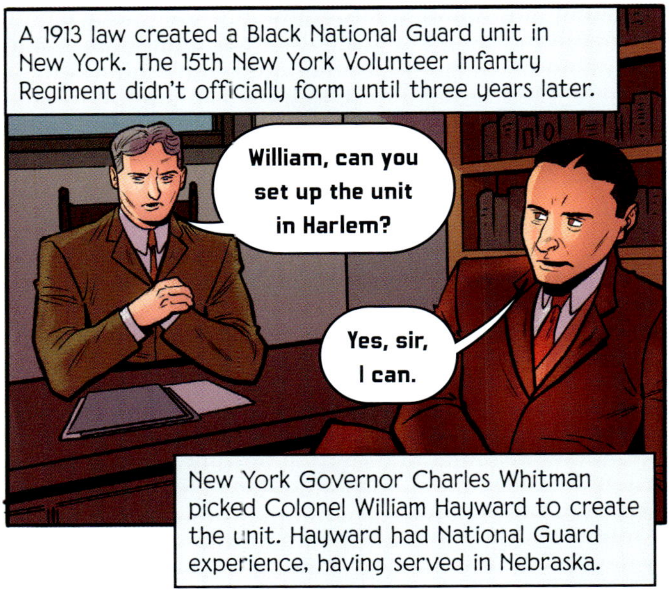
A 1913 law created a Black National Guard unit in New York. The 15th New York Volunteer Infantry Regiment didn't officially form until three years later.
William, can you set up the unit in Harlem?
Yes, sir, I can.
New York Governor Charles Whitman picked Colonel William Hayward to create the unit. Hayward had National Guard experience, having served in Nebraska.

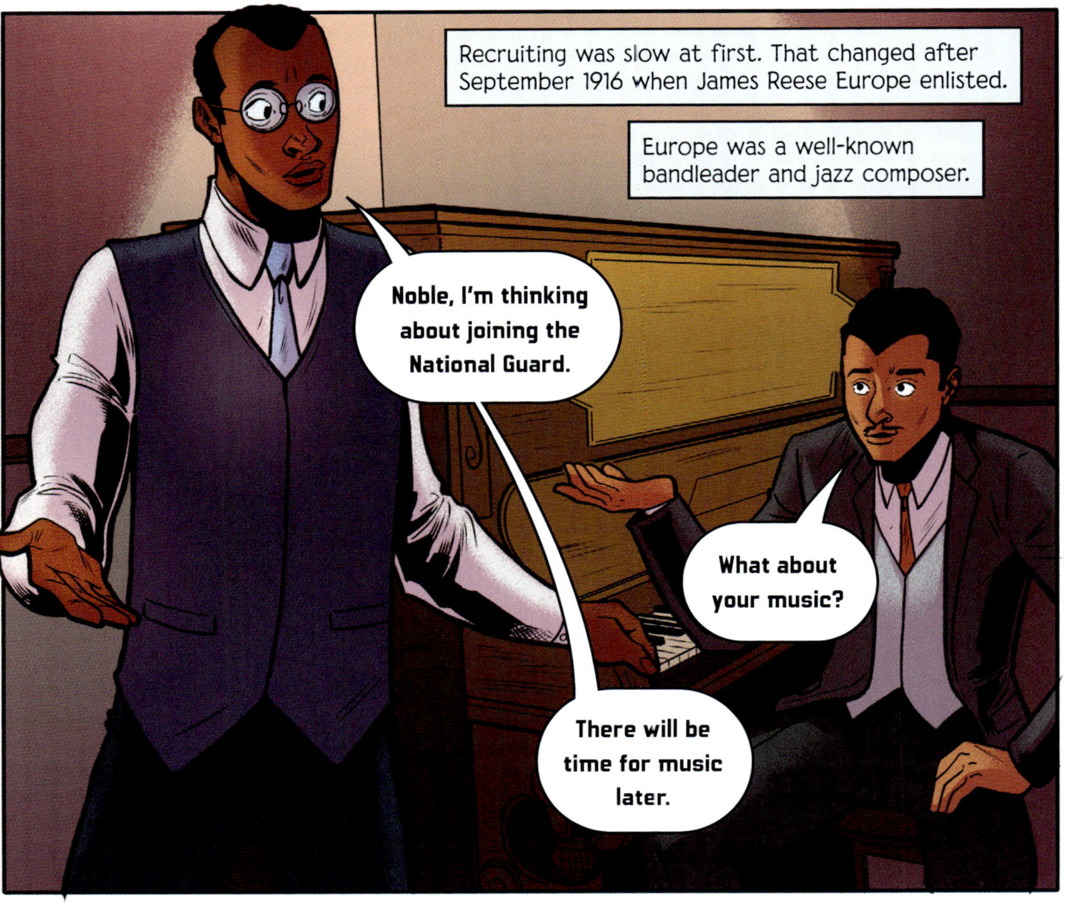
Recruiting was slow at first. That changed after September 1916 when James Reese Europe enlisted.
Europe was a well-known bandleader and jazz composer.
Noble, I'm thinking about joining the National Guard.
What about your music?
There will be time for music later.

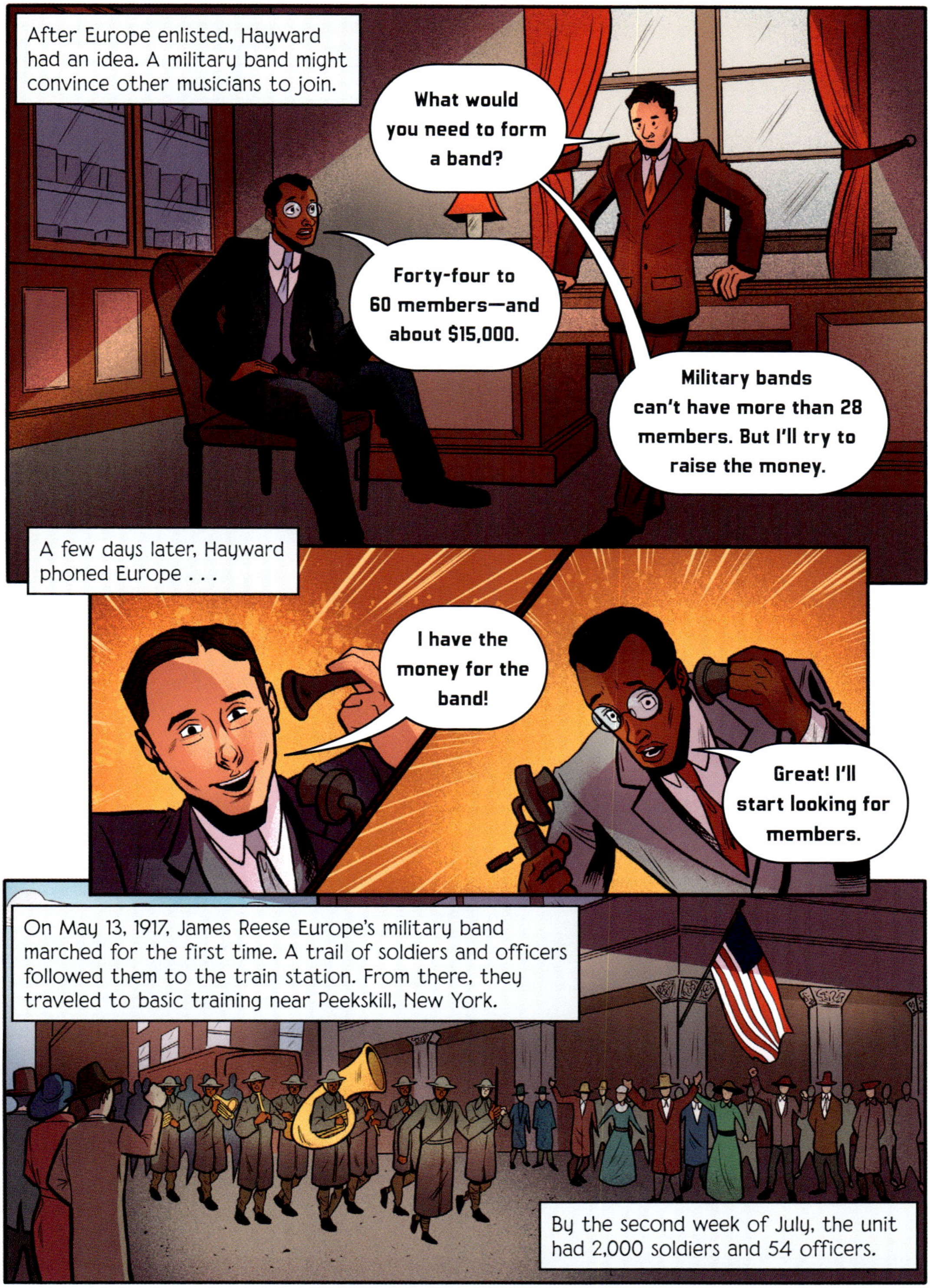

After Europe enlisted, Hayward had an idea. A military band might convince other musicians to join.
What would you need to form a band?
Forty-four to 60 members—and about $15,000.
Military bands can't have more than 28 members. But I'll try to raise the money.
A few days later, Hayward phoned Europe . . .
I have the money for the band!
Great! I'll start looking for members.
On May 13, 1917, James Reese Europe's military band marched for the first time. A trail of soldiers and officers followed them to the train station. From there, they traveled to basic training near Peekskill, New York.
By the second week of July, the unit had 2,000 soldiers and 54 officers.

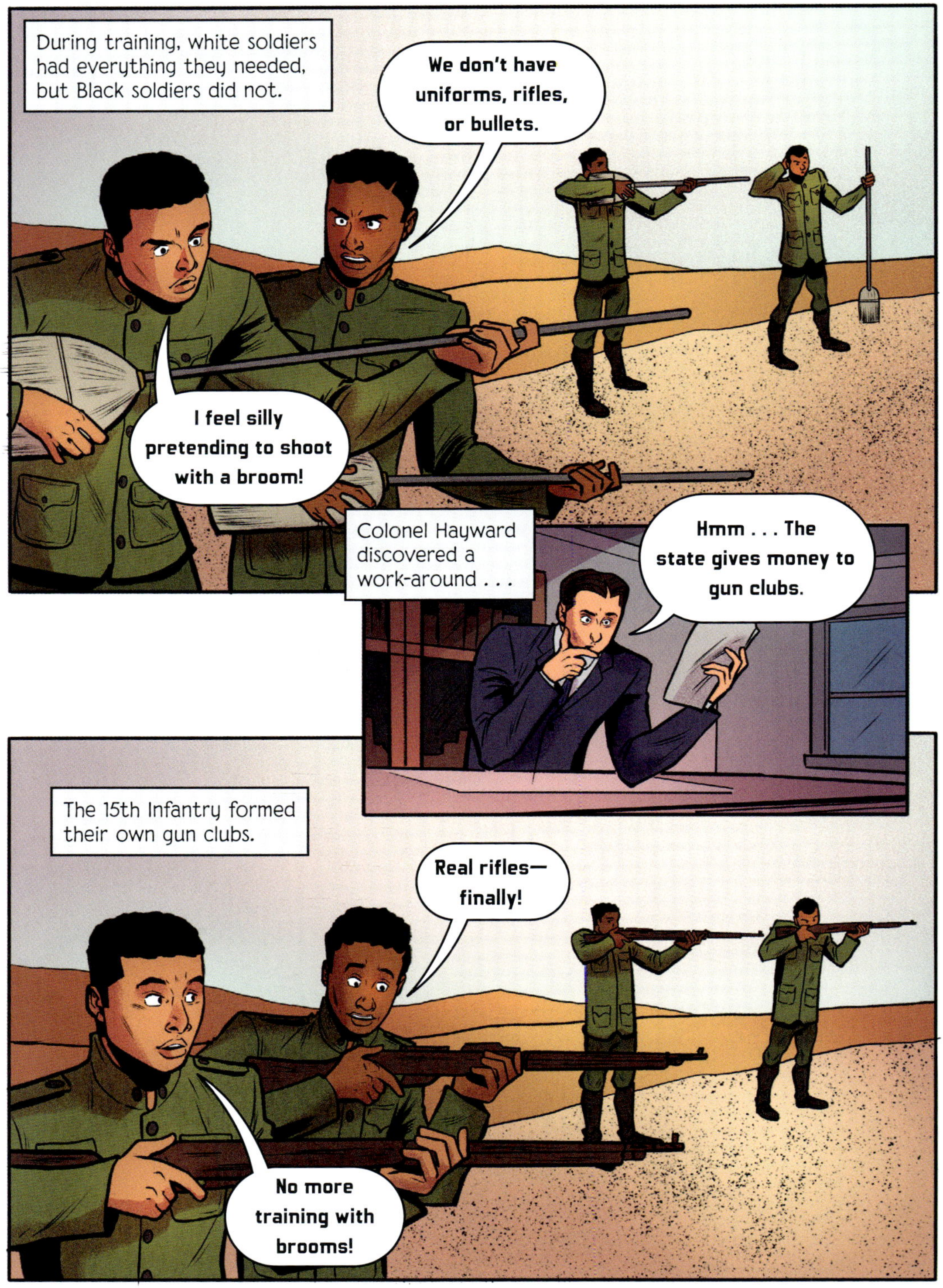
During training, white soldiers had everything they needed, but Black soldiers did not.
We don't have uniforms, rifles, or bullets.
I feel silly pretending to shoot with a broom!
Colonel Hayward discovered a work-around . . .
Hmm . . . The state gives money to gun clubs.
The 15th Infantry formed their own gun clubs.
Real rifles—finally!
No more training with brooms!

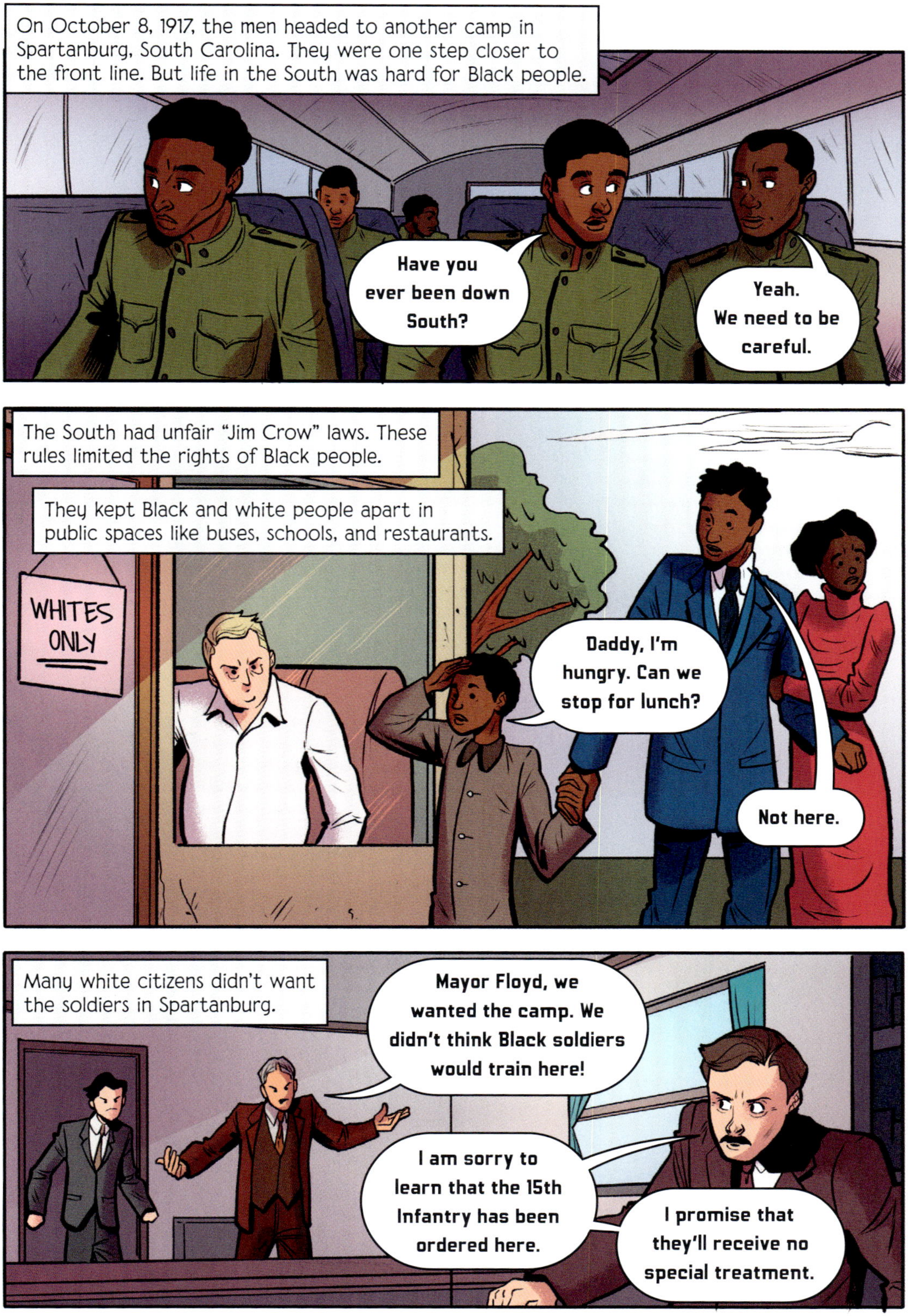
On October 8, 1917, the men headed to another camp in Spartanburg, South Carolina. They were one step closer to the front line. But life in the South was hard for Black people.
Have you ever been down South?
Yeah. We need to be careful.
The South had unfair "Jim Crow" laws. These rules limited the rights of Black people.
They kept Black and white people apart in public spaces like buses, schools, and restaurants.
WHITES ONLY
Daddy, I'm hungry. Can we stop for lunch?
Not here.
Many white citizens didn't want the soldiers in Spartanburg.
Mayor Floyd, we wanted the camp. We didn't think Black soldiers would train here!
I am sorry to learn that the 15th Infantry has been ordered here.
I promise that they'll receive no special treatment.

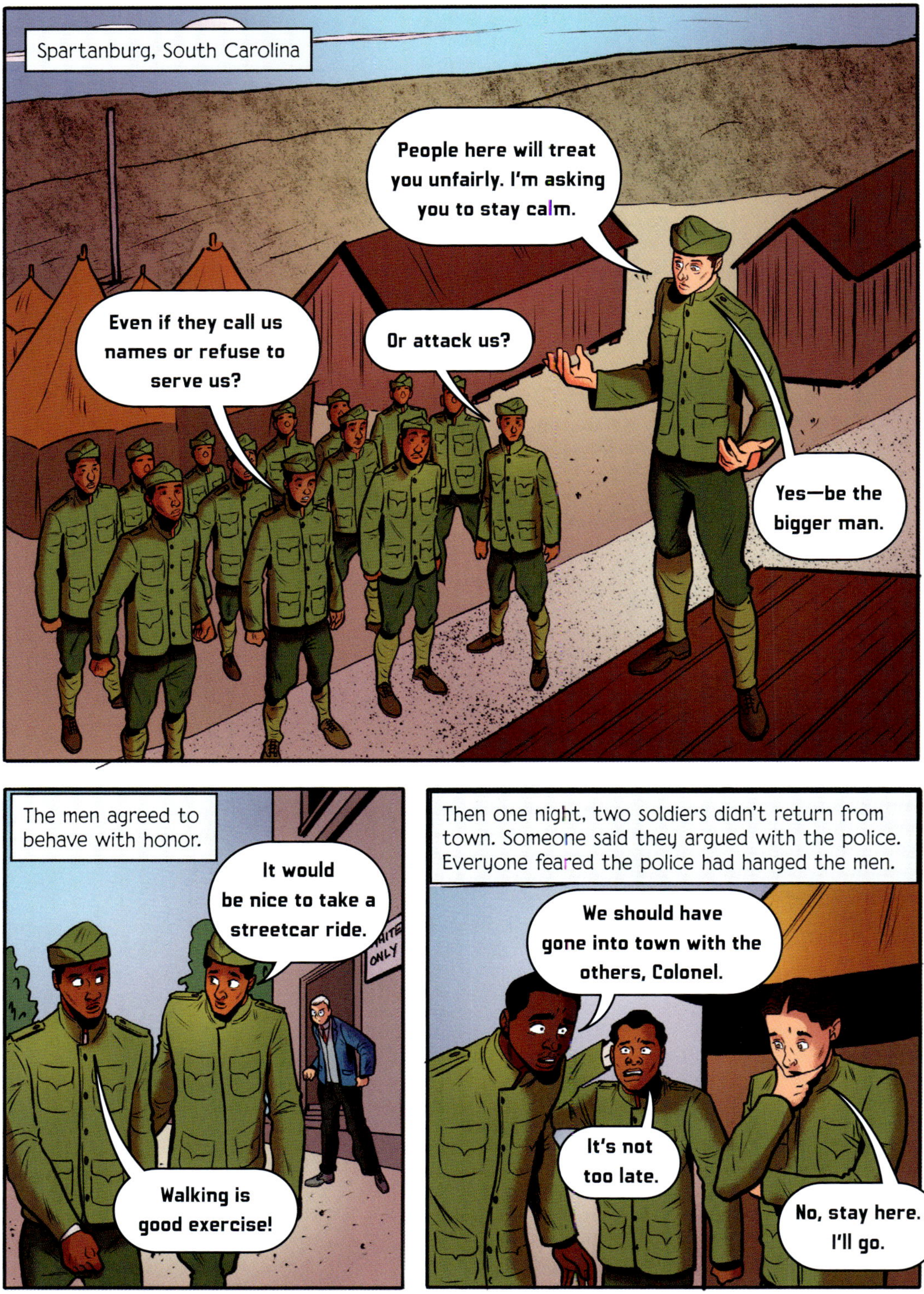
Spartanburg, South Carolina
People here will treat you unfairly. I'm asking you to stay calm.
Even if they call us names or refuse to serve us?
Or attack us?
Yes—be the bigger man.
The men agreed to behave with honor.
It would be nice to take a streetcar ride.
Walking is good exercise!
ONLY
Then one night, two soldiers didn't return from town. Someone said they argued with the police. Everyone feared the police had hanged the men.
We should have gone into town with the others, Colonel.
It's not too late.
No, stay here. I'll go.

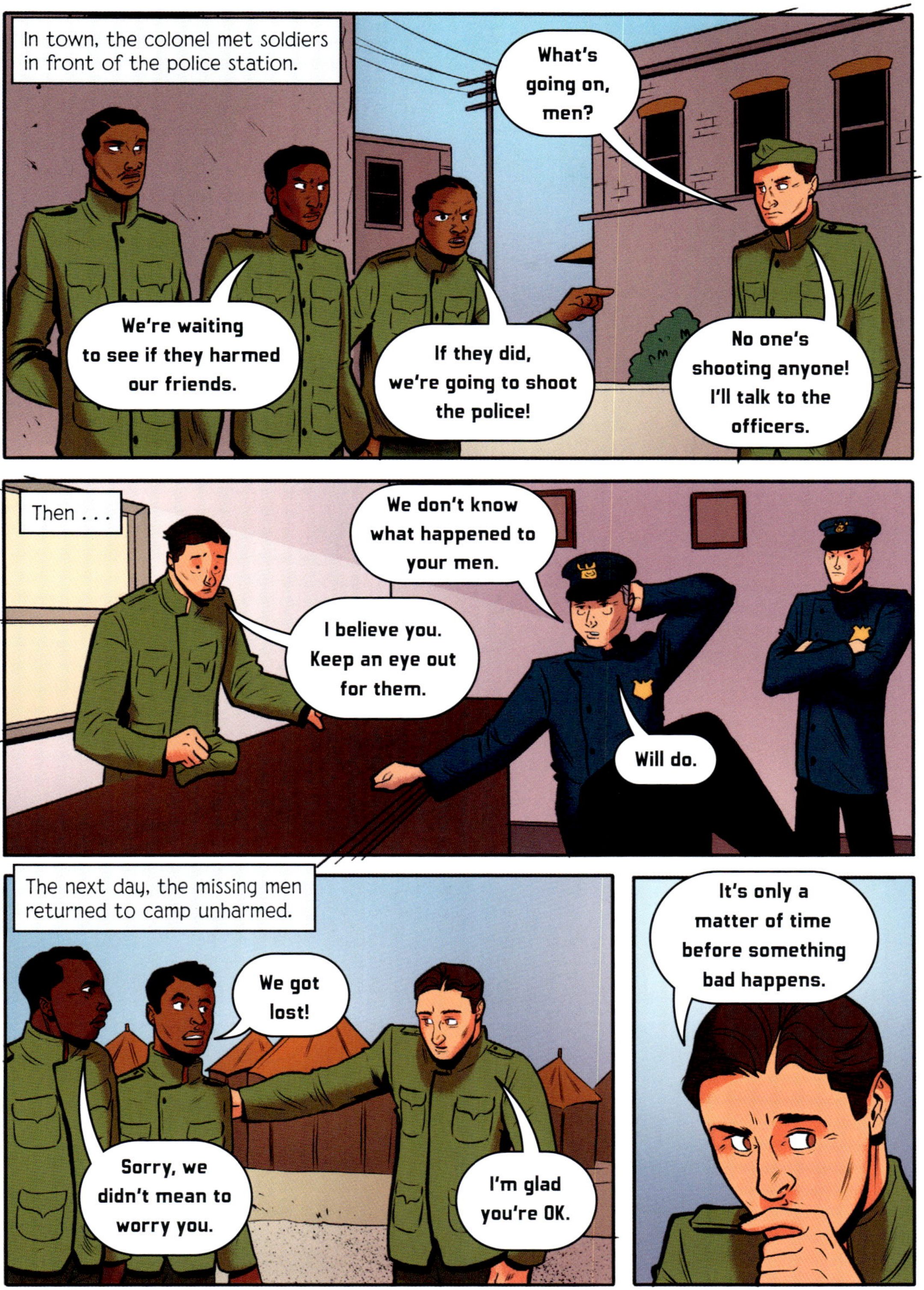
In town, the colonel met soldiers in front of the police station.
What's going on, men?
We're waiting to see if they harmed our friends.
If they did, we're going to shoot the police!
No one's shooting anyone! I'll talk to the officers.
Then . . .
We don't know what happened to your men.
I believe you. Keep an eye out for them.
Will do.
The next day, the missing men returned to camp unharmed.
We got lost!
Sorry, we didn't mean to worry you.
I'm glad you're OK.
It's only a matter of time before something bad happens.

CHAPTER THREE: THE FRENCH CONNECTION

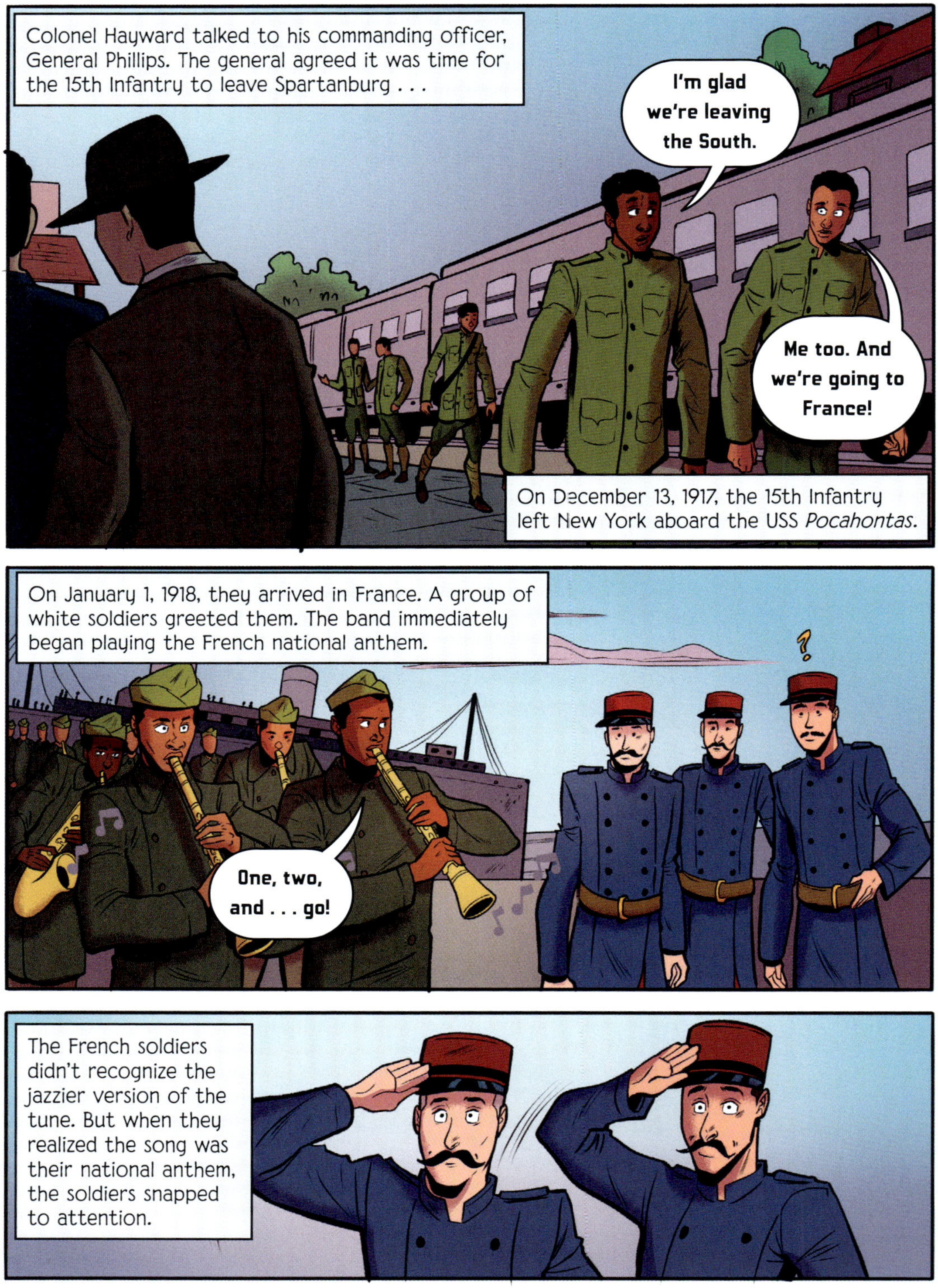
Colonel Hayward talked to his commanding officer, General Phillips. The general agreed it was time for the 15th Infantry to leave Spartanburg . . .
I'm glad we're leaving the South.
Me too. And we're going to France!
On December 13, 1917, the 15th Infantry left New York aboard the USS *Pocahontas*.
On January 1, 1918, they arrived in France. A group of white soldiers greeted them. The band immediately began playing the French national anthem.
?
One, two, and . . . go!
The French soldiers didn't recognize the jazzier version of the tune. But when they realized the song was their national anthem, the soldiers snapped to attention.

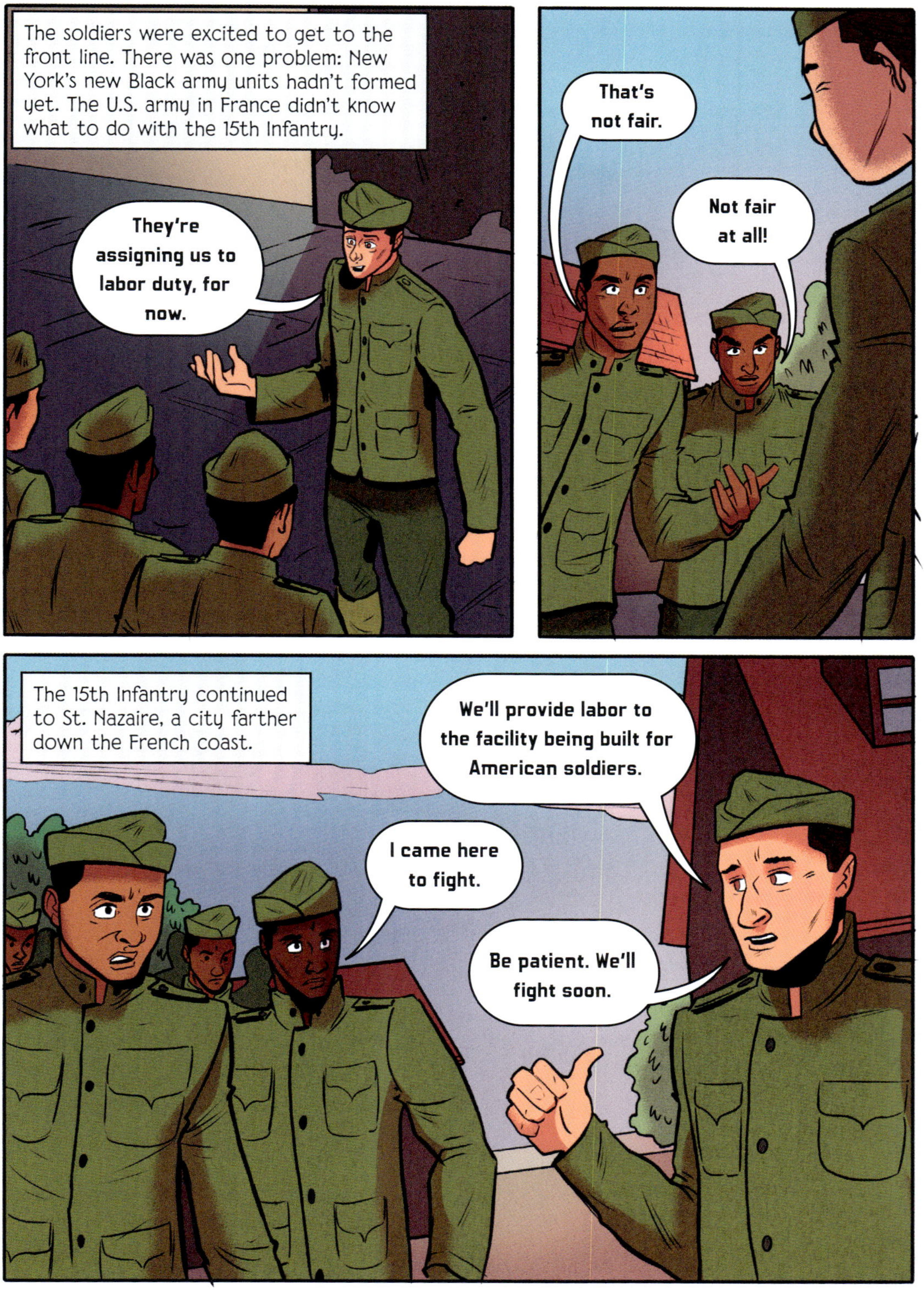
The soldiers were excited to get to the front line. There was one problem: New York's new Black army units hadn't formed yet. The U.S. army in France didn't know what to do with the 15th Infantry.
They're assigning us to labor duty, for now.
That's not fair.
Not fair at all!
The 15th Infantry continued to St. Nazaire, a city farther down the French coast.
We'll provide labor to the facility being built for American soldiers.
I came here to fight.
Be patient. We'll fight soon.

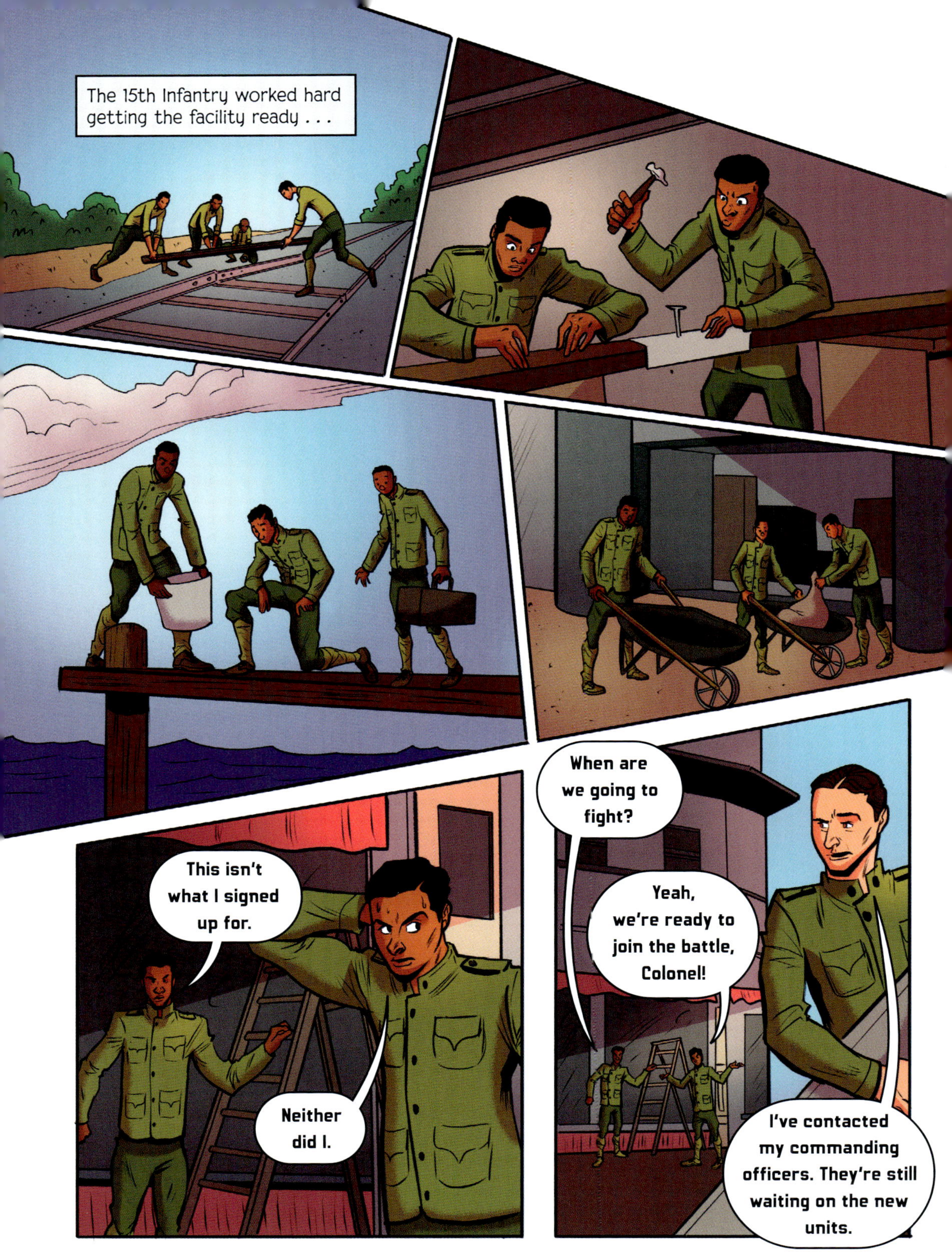
The 15th Infantry worked hard getting the facility ready . . .
This isn't what I signed up for.
Neither did I.
When are we going to fight?
Yeah, we're ready to join the battle, Colonel!
I've contacted my commanding officers. They're still waiting on the new units.

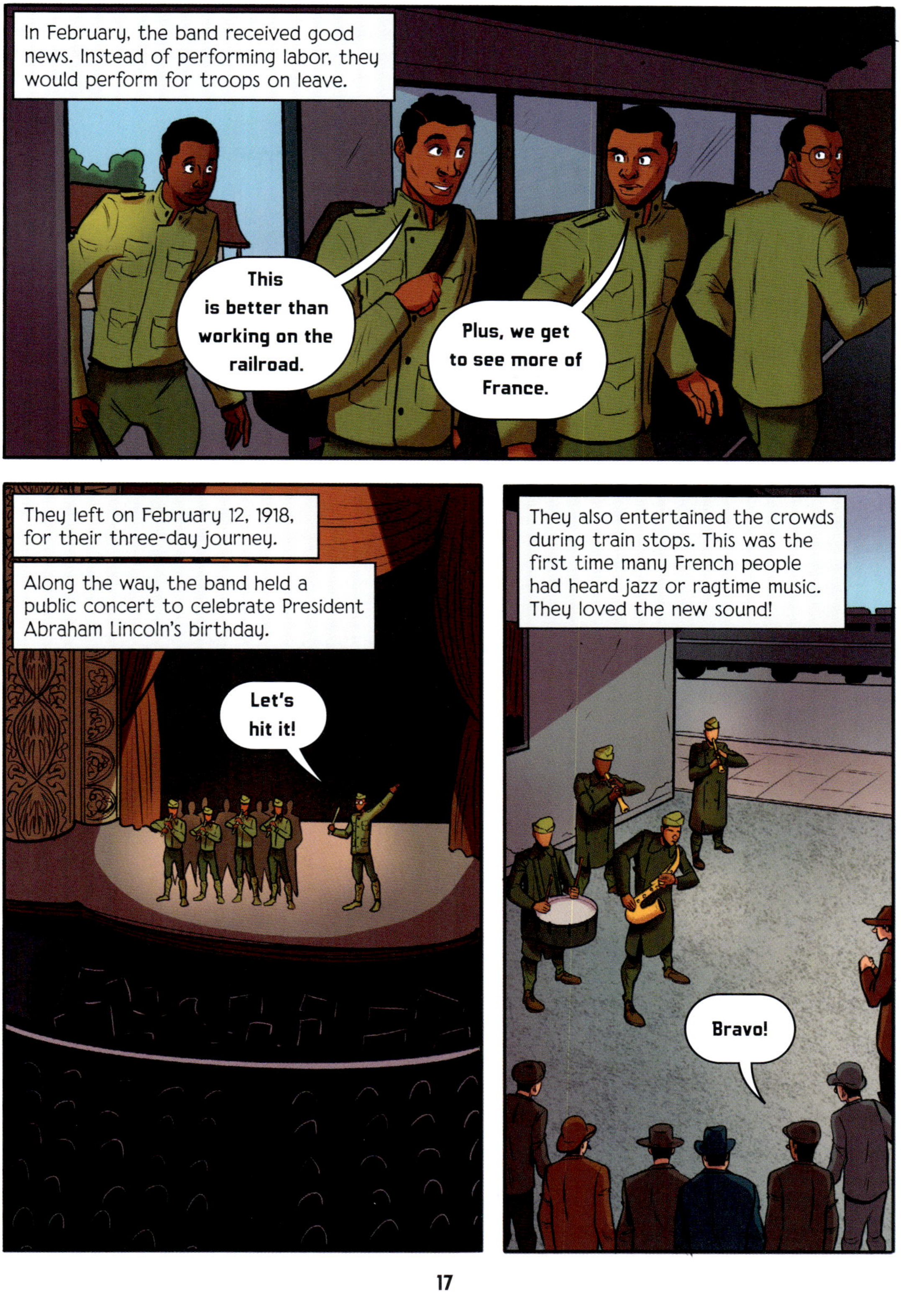
In February, the band received good news. Instead of performing labor, they would perform for troops on leave.
This is better than working on the railroad.
Plus, we get to see more of France.
They left on February 12, 1918, for their three-day journey.
Along the way, the band held a public concert to celebrate President Abraham Lincoln's birthday.
Let's hit it!
They also entertained the crowds during train stops. This was the first time many French people had heard jazz or ragtime music. They loved the new sound!
Bravo!

In the meantime, Colonel Hayward was given two choices. One, the 15th Infantry could return to the U.S. and wait for the creation of the Black units. He went with the second choice . . .
Good news—we're being attached to the French army!
The French already had Black troops. They were happy to have more.
The 15th Infantry became the first U.S. troops to join a French army unit. They were also the first Black soldiers to do so.
This is great news!
Woo-hoo! No more labor for us.
During the first week of March, the 15th Infantry joined the 16th Division of the 4th French Army. They were renamed the 369th Infantry Regiment.
During training, the soldiers learned some useful French words.
Retomber.
Fall back.
They learned to use French weapons.
Why do we have to use French rifles?
We don't have American bullets.

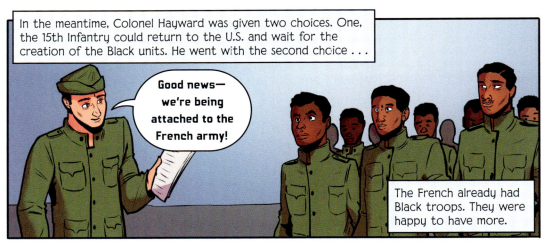

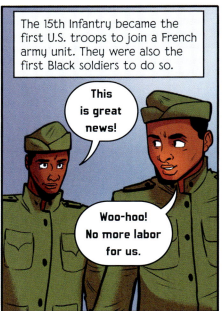

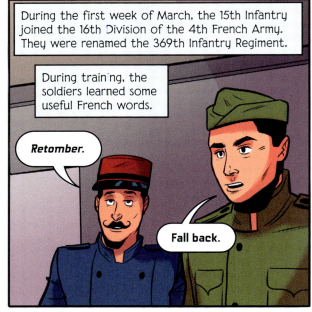

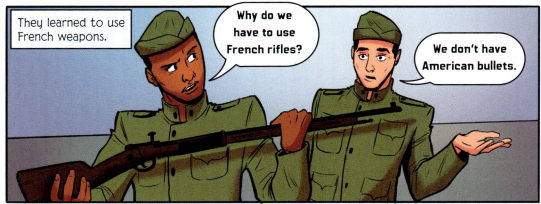

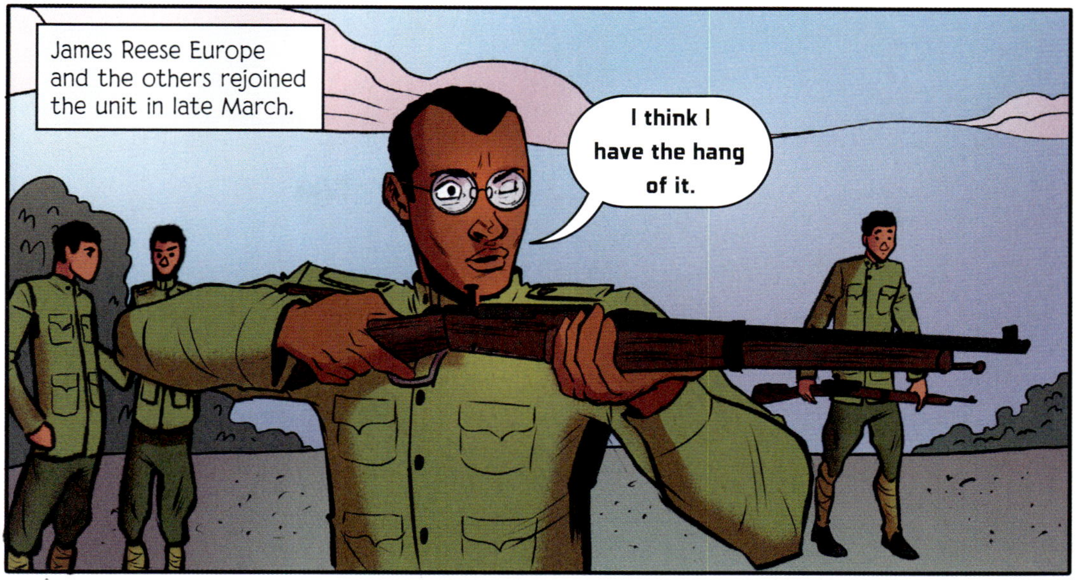
James Reese Europe and the others rejoined the unit in late March.
I think I have the hang of it.

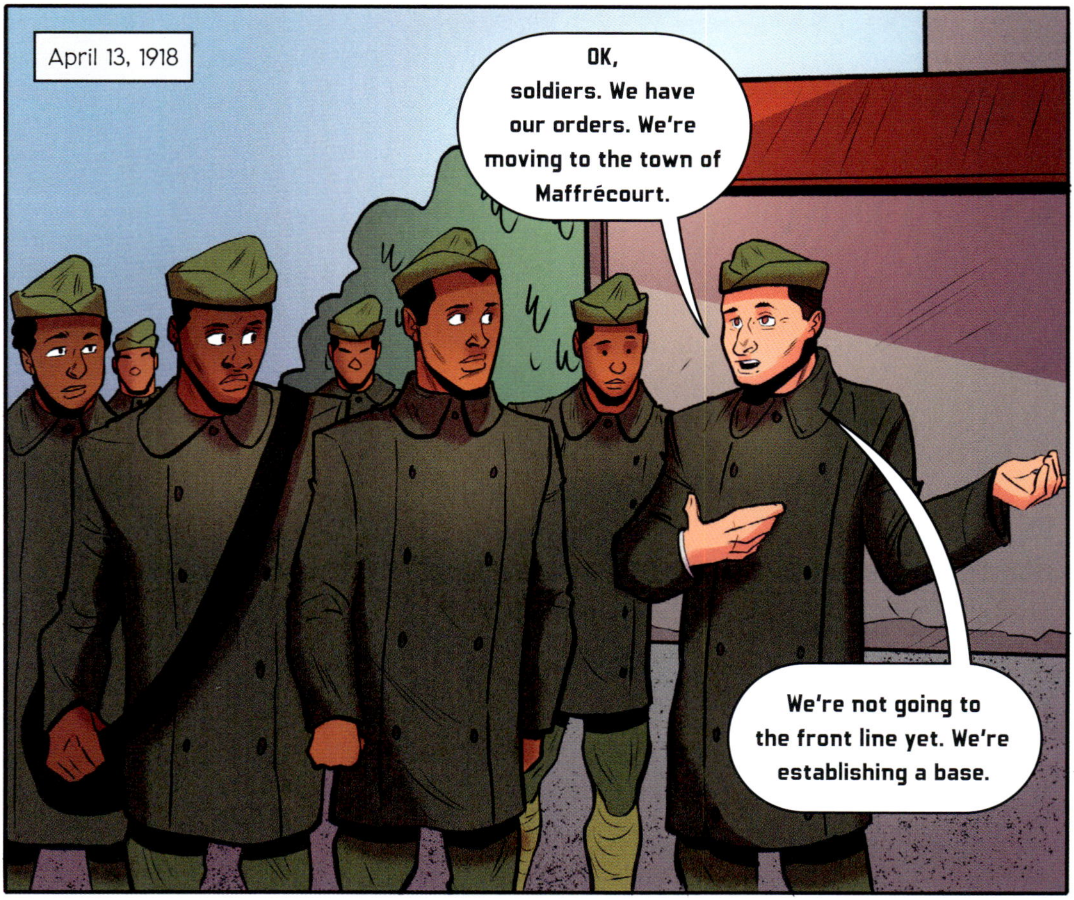
April 13, 1918
OK, soldiers. We have our orders. We're moving to the town of Maffrécourt.
We're not going to the front line yet. We're establishing a base.

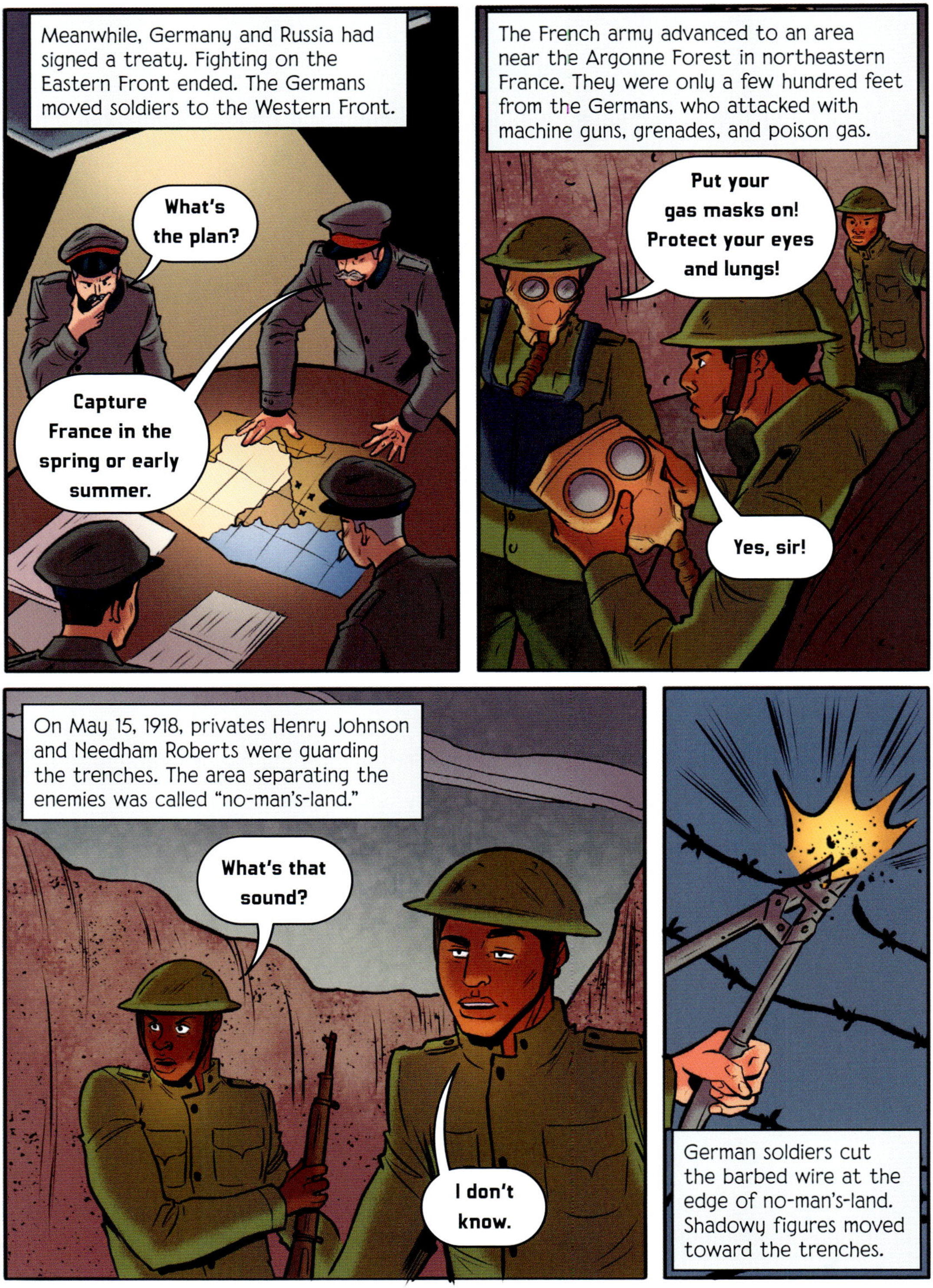
Meanwhile, Germany and Russia had signed a treaty. Fighting on the Eastern Front ended. The Germans moved soldiers to the Western Front.
What's the plan?
Capture France in the spring or early summer.
The French army advanced to an area near the Argonne Forest in northeastern France. They were only a few hundred feet from the Germans, who attacked with machine guns, grenades, and poison gas.
Put your gas masks on! Protect your eyes and lungs!
Yes, sir!
On May 15, 1918, privates Henry Johnson and Needham Roberts were guarding the trenches. The area separating the enemies was called "no-man's-land."
What's that sound?
I don't know.
German soldiers cut the barbed wire at the edge of no-man's-land. Shadowy figures moved toward the trenches.

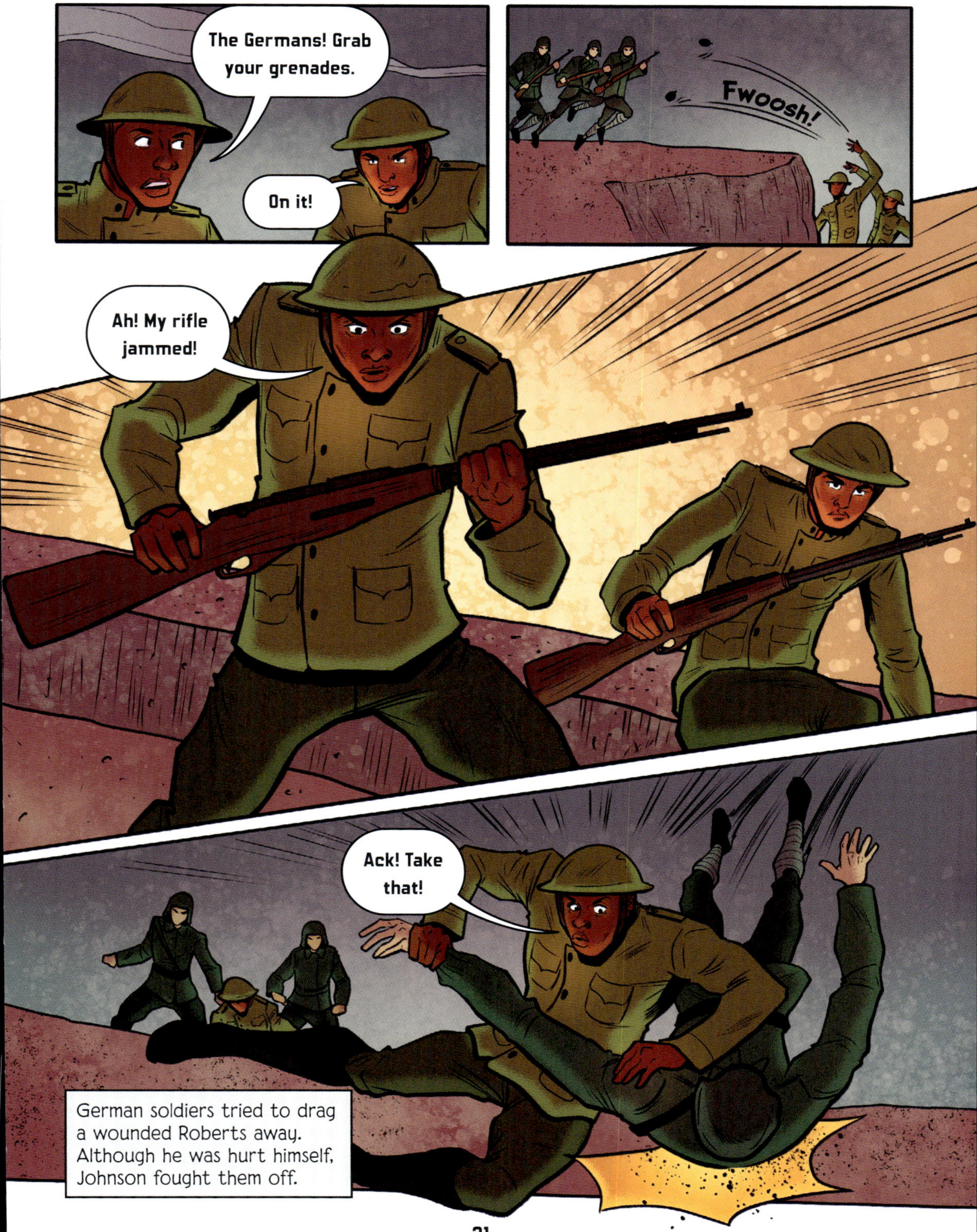
The Germans! Grab your grenades.
On it!
Fwoosh!
Ah! My rifle jammed!
Ack! Take that!
German soldiers tried to drag a wounded Roberts away. Although he was hurt himself, Johnson fought them off.

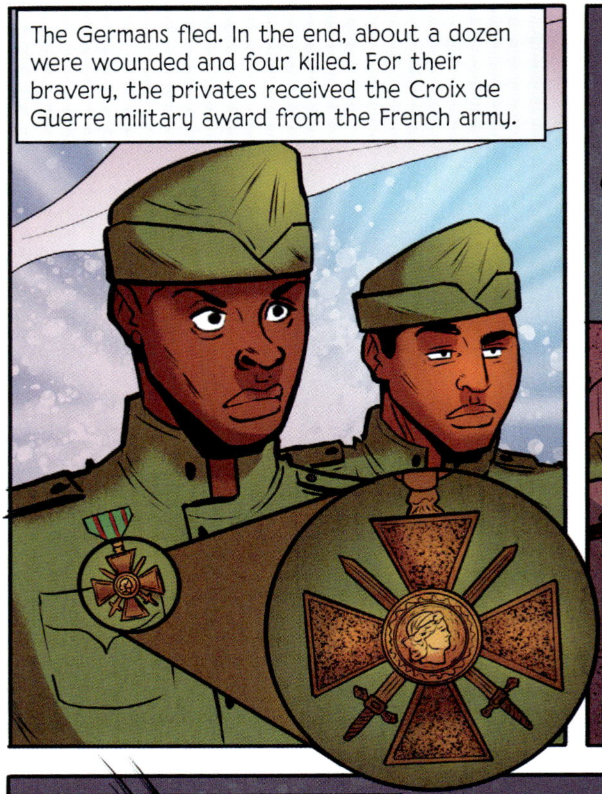
The Germans fled. In the end, about a dozen were wounded and four killed. For their bravery, the privates received the Croix de Guerre military award from the French army.

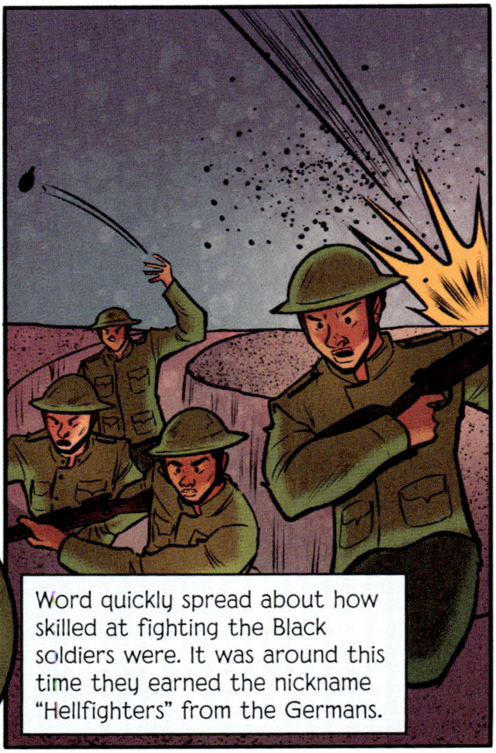
Word quickly spread about how skilled at fighting the Black soldiers were. It was around this time they earned the nickname "Hellfighters" from the Germans.

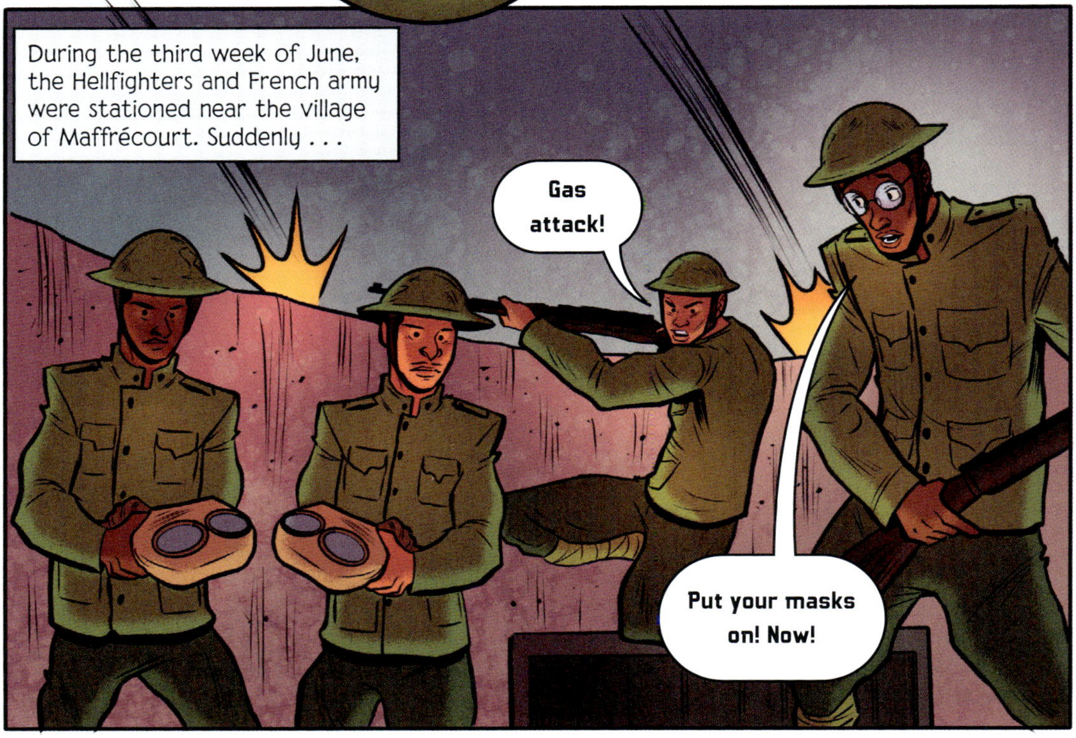
During the third week of June, the Hellfighters and French army were stationed near the village of Maffrécourt. Suddenly . . .
Gas attack!
Put your masks on! Now!

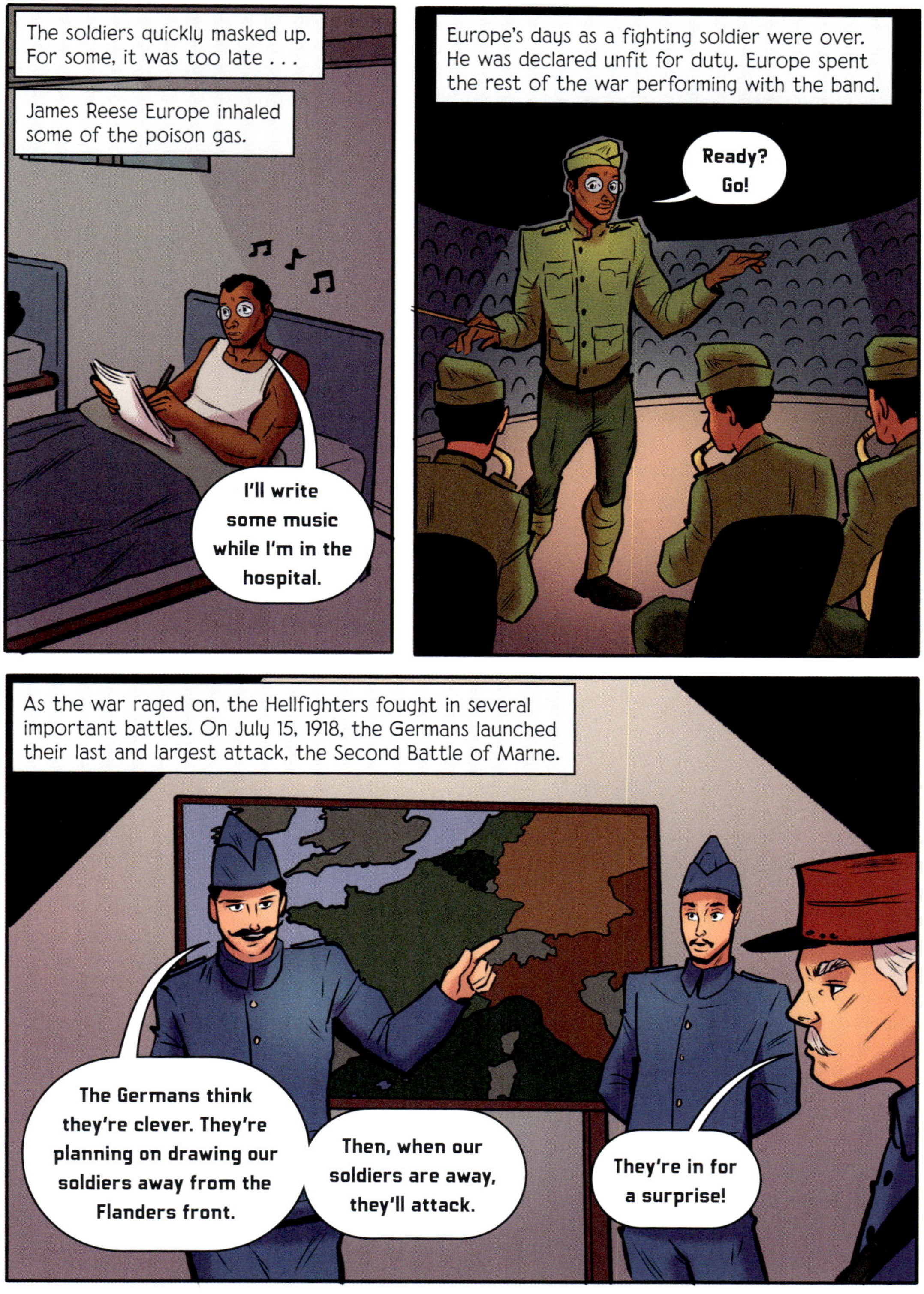

The soldiers quickly masked up. For some, it was too late . . .
James Reese Europe inhaled some of the poison gas.
I'll write some music while I'm in the hospital.
Europe's days as a fighting soldier were over. He was declared unfit for duty. Europe spent the rest of the war performing with the band.
Ready? Go!
As the war raged on, the Hellfighters fought in several important battles. On July 15, 1918, the Germans launched their last and largest attack, the Second Battle of Marne.
The Germans think they're clever. They're planning on drawing our soldiers away from the Flanders front.
Then, when our soldiers are away, they'll attack.
They're in for a surprise!

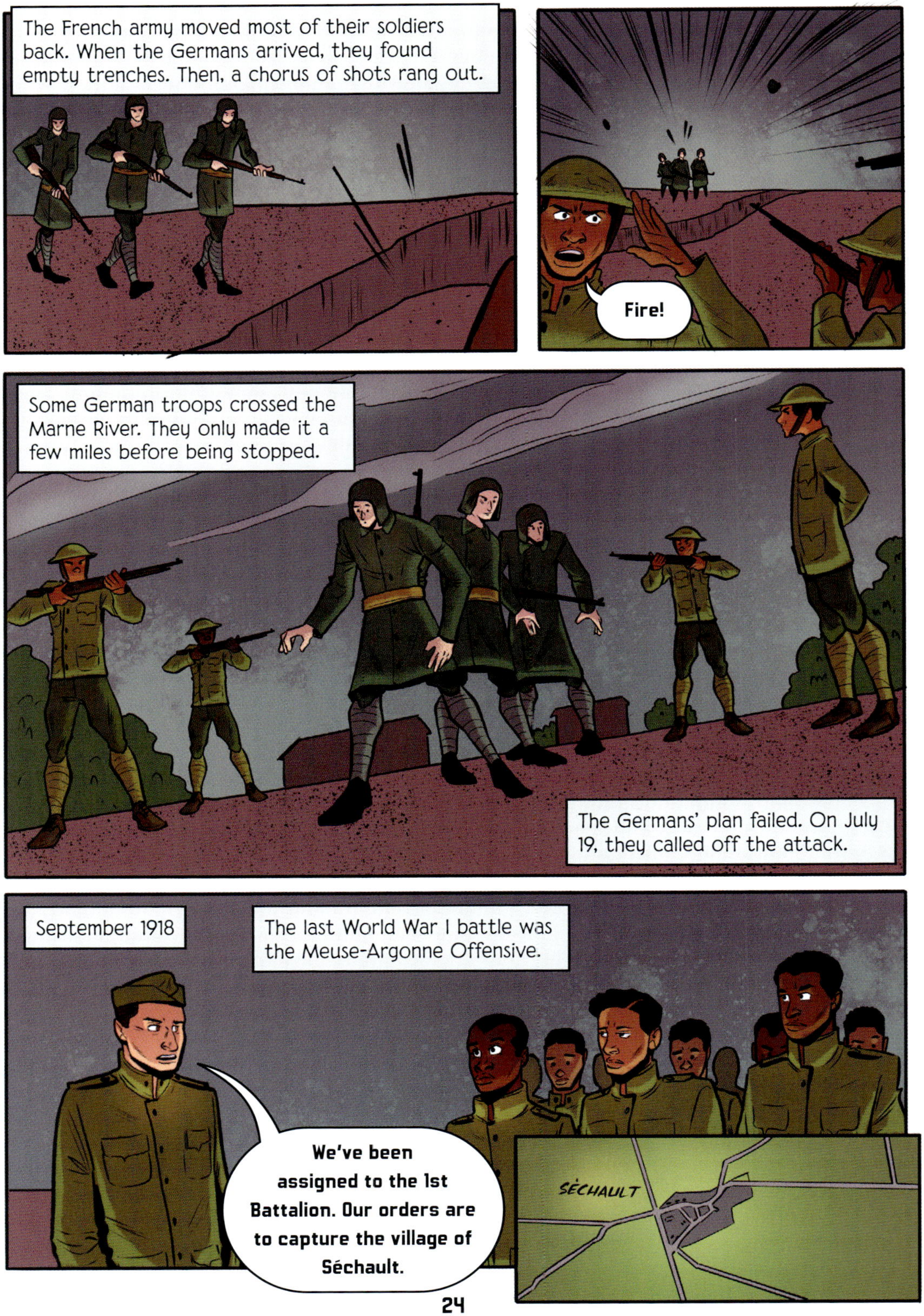
The French army moved most of their soldiers back. When the Germans arrived, they found empty trenches. Then, a chorus of shots rang out.
Fire!
Some German troops crossed the Marne River. They only made it a few miles before being stopped.
The Germans' plan failed. On July 19, they called off the attack.
September 1918
The last World War I battle was the Meuse-Argonne Offensive.
We've been assigned to the 1st Battalion. Our orders are to capture the village of Séchault.
SÉCHAULT

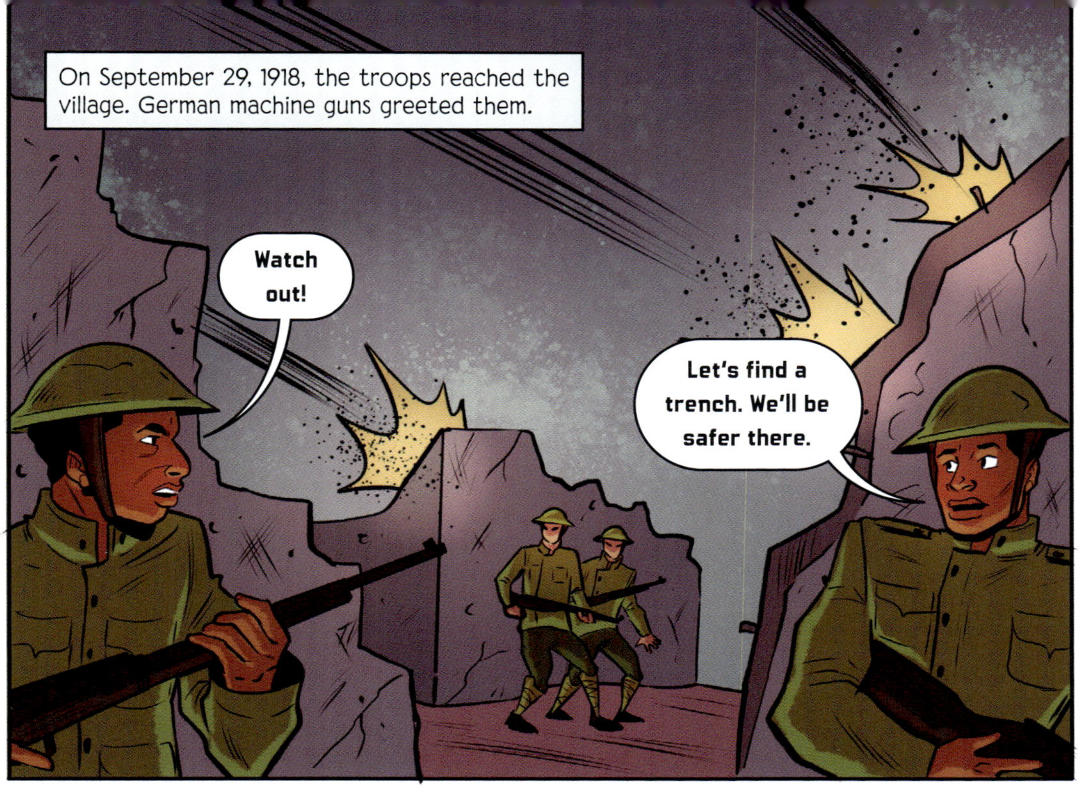
On September 29, 1918, the troops reached the village. German machine guns greeted them.
Watch out!
Let's find a trench. We'll be safer there.

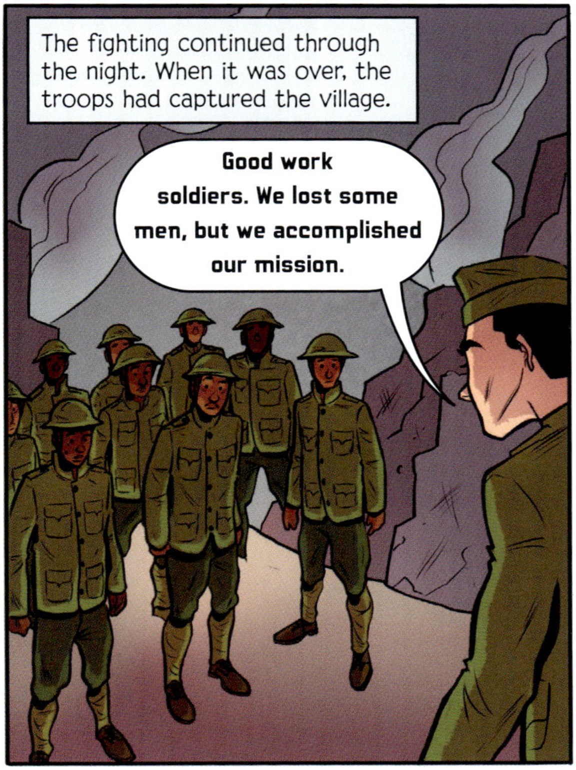
The fighting continued through the night. When it was over, the troops had captured the village.
Good work soldiers. We lost some men, but we accomplished our mission.

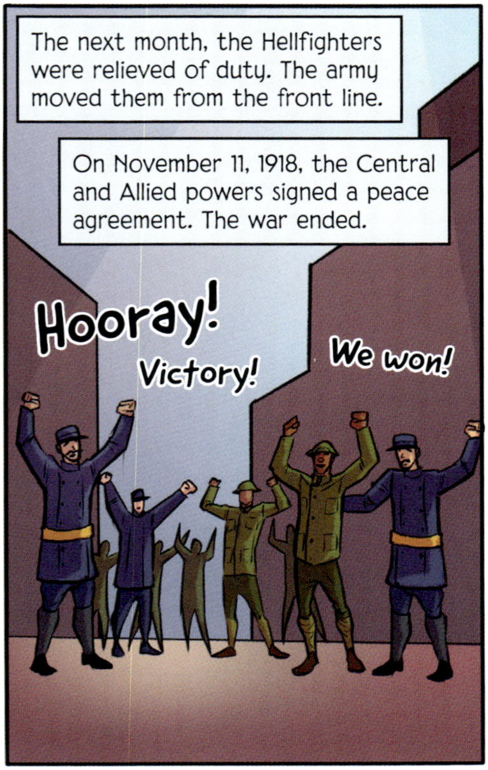
The next month, the Hellfighters were relieved of duty. The army moved them from the front line.
On November 11, 1918, the Central and Allied powers signed a peace agreement. The war ended.
Hooray!
Victory!
We won!

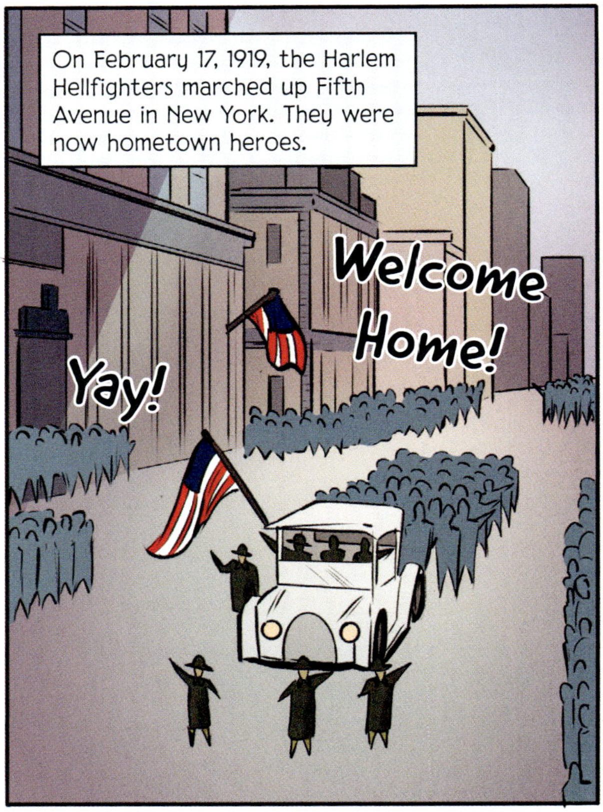
On February 17, 1919, the Harlem Hellfighters marched up Fifth Avenue in New York. They were now hometown heroes.
Welcome Home!
Yay!

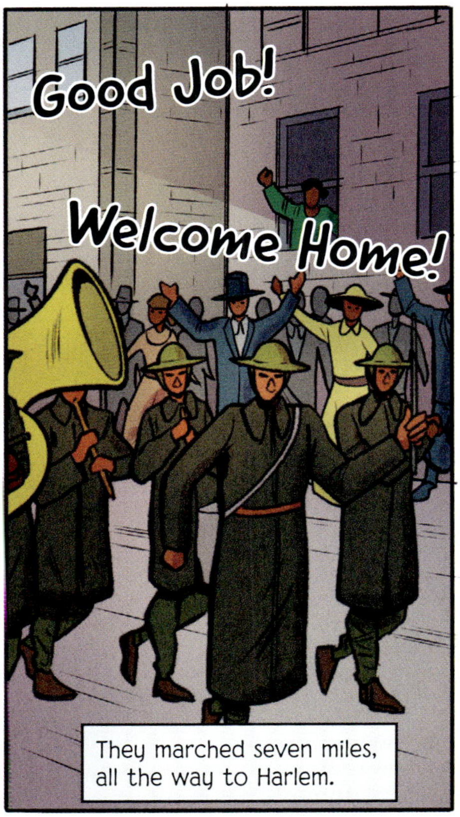
Good Job!
Welcome Home!
They marched seven miles, all the way to Harlem.

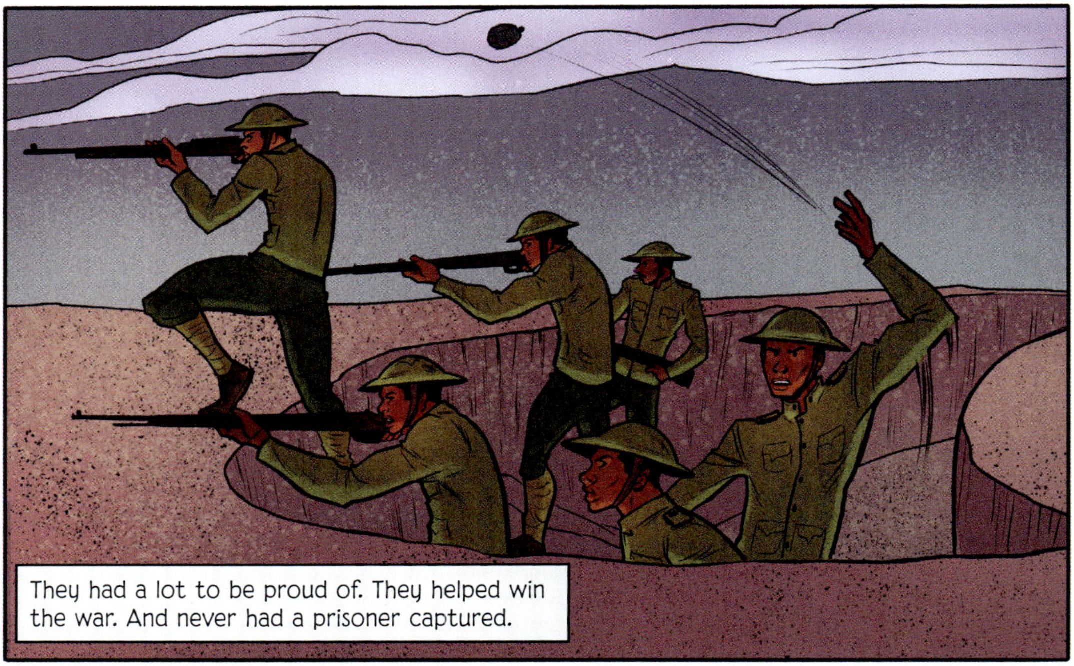
They had a lot to be proud of. They helped win the war. And never had a prisoner captured.

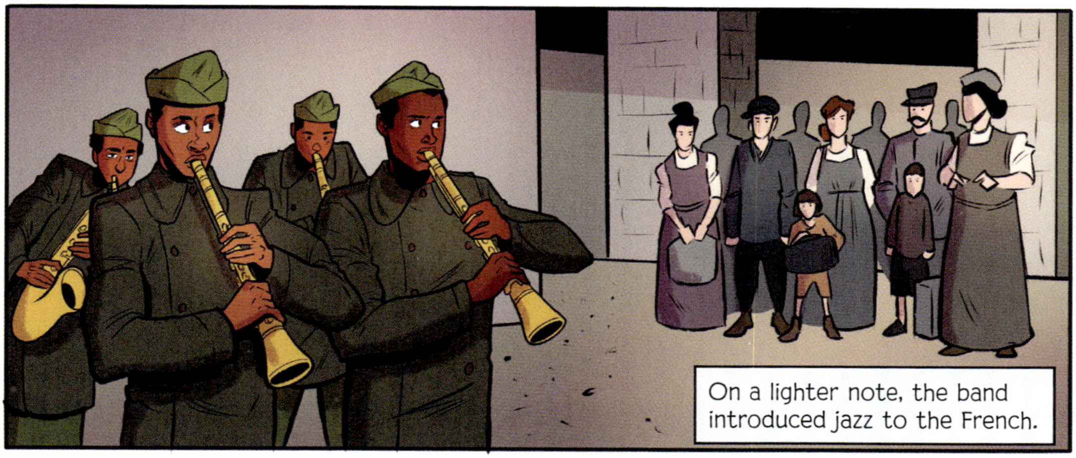
On a lighter note, the band introduced jazz to the French.

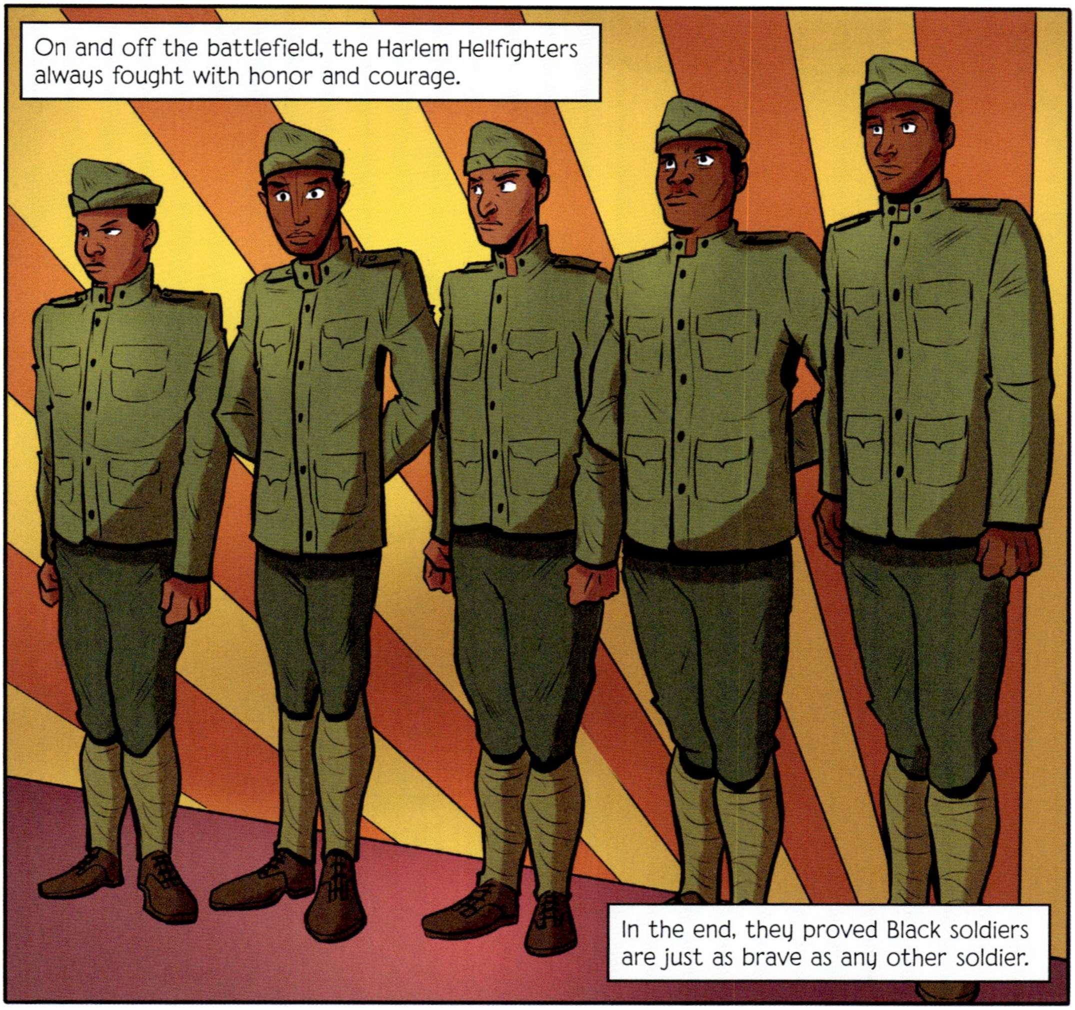
On and off the battlefield, the Harlem Hellfighters always fought with honor and courage.
In the end, they proved Black soldiers are just as brave as any other soldier.

MORE ABOUT THE HARLEM HELLFIGHTERS OF WORLD WAR I

- National Guard units are civilians with military training. They provide support but aren't part of the military branches. These men and women often work or attend college while training. Many live and work in their home state. They don't live on military bases unless called to active duty.

- Most of the money for the 15th Infantry's band came from one person: wealthy businessman Daniel G. Reid. He gave Colonel Hayward $10,000 to start the band.

- Their band played throughout France and is credited with introducing jazz to the French and British.

- Although the French government rewarded the Hellfighters for their bravery, the U.S. Army did not award any medals to the unit.
- The Hellfighters spent more time in continuous combat—191 days—than any other U.S. military unit.
- In 2015, 86 years after he died, Henry Johnson was awarded the Medal of Honor by President Barack Obama.

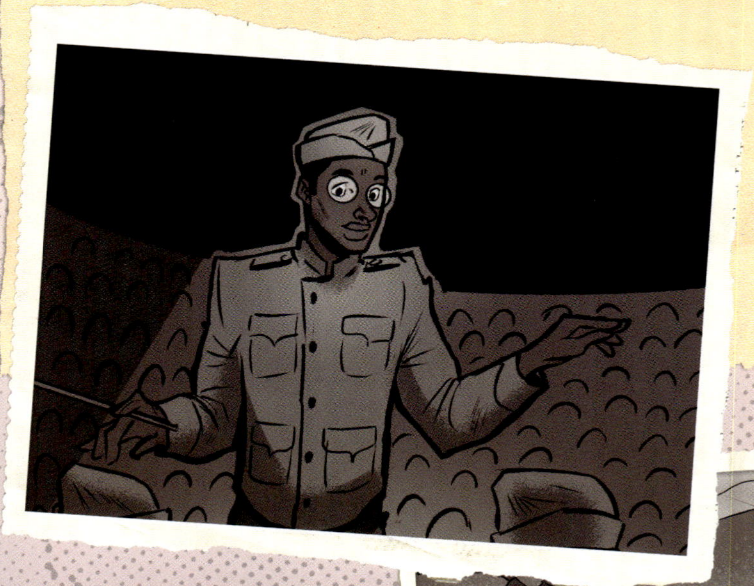

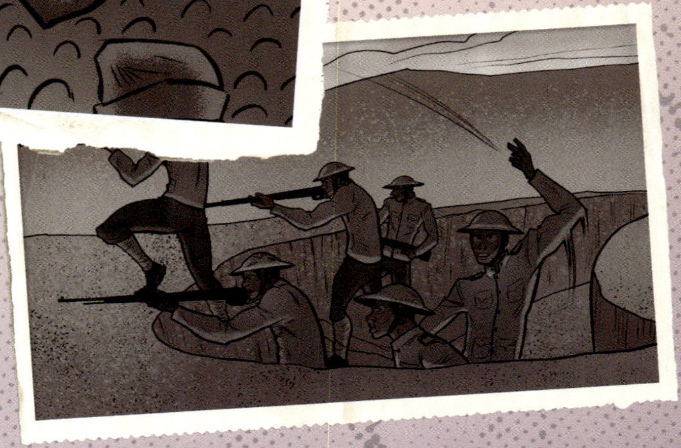

GLOSSARY

front line (FRUHNT LYN)—a military line formed by the most advanced tactical combat units

heir (AYR)—a person who is next in line to receive something, like a title or property, often after someone dies

infantry (IN-fun-tree)—soldiers who fight on foot

jazz (JAZ)—a type of lively music that started in the United States, often using instruments like trumpets and saxophones

mayday (may-DAY)—an international radio signal word used as a distress call

merchant (MUR-chuhnt)—of, relating to, or used in trade

ragtime (RAYG-tym)—music played with a strong march-style rhythm and a lively melody with accented notes falling on beats that are not usually accented

regiment (REJ-uh-ment)—a large group of soldiers that is part of an army

trench (TRENCH)—a ditch protected by a bank of earth used to shelter soldiers

READ MORE

Braun, Eric. *Can You Survive a World War I Escape?* North Mankato, MN: Capstone, 2023.

Medina, Nico. *What Was World War I?* New York: Penguin Workshop, 2023.

Micklos, John Jr. *Harlem Hellfighters.* North Mankato, MN: Capstone 2019.

INTERNET SITES

National Museum of African American History & Culture: Our American Story: Remembering the Harlem Hellfighters
nmaahc.si.edu/explore/stories/remembering-harlem-hellfighters

National Park Service: Who Are They? Men in the 369th Infantry Iconic Photo
nps.gov/articles/000/iconic369thphoto.htm

PBS: Who Were the Harlem Hellfighters?
pbs.org/wnet/african-americans-many-rivers-to-cross/history/who-were-the-harlem-hellfighters

OTHER TITLES IN THE SERIES:

ELITE MILITARY UNITS
BUSHMASTERS
ELITE COMBAT TEAM of World War II

ELITE MILITARY UNITS
CHOCTAW CODE TALKERS
ELITE SECRET MESSENGERS of World War I

ELITE MILITARY UNITS
NISEI SOLDIERS
ELITE FIGHTING FORCE of World War II

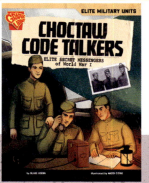

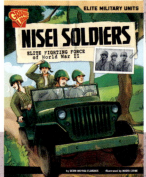

ABOUT THE AUTHOR

Myra Faye Turner is a New Orleans-based poet and author. She has written for grown-ups but prefers writing for young readers. She has written four dozen fiction and nonfiction books for children and young adults. Her favorite topics to write about include lesser-known historical Black figures and events, science, and interesting or unusual animals. She also enjoys writing reader's theater and fable retellings. When not writing, she spends her days reading, napping, and drinking coffee.

ABOUT THE ILLUSTRATOR

Colombian-born artist Orlando Caicedo grew up eating arepas and drawing. Since completing his BFA at the Atlanta College of Art, his work has included the critically acclaimed graphic novel *Colin Kaepernick: Change the Game* (Graphix), *The Badguys and Pound* (Webtoon), and *Dryfoot* (Mad Cave Studios). When not drawing comics, he can be found napping with his loving wife and two adorable daughters.